short i

Sounds & Letters 3

KNOWLEDGE BOOKS

lid	pig
dig	pin
bin	pip
lip	

lid

2

3

pig

dig

pin

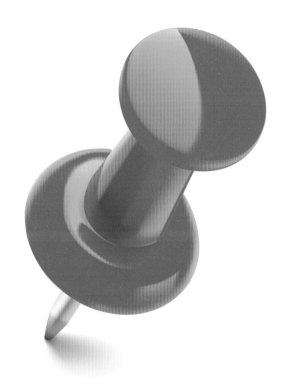

bin

11

pip

13

lip

lid	pig
dig	pin
bin	pip
lip	

Knowledge Books and Software
PO Box 50 Sandgate, Queensland 4017 Australia
p. +617-55680288 f. +617-55680277 email: sales@kbs.com.au

First Published 2022
ISBN 9781922516756
Text and editing: Carole Crimeen
Design and layout: Suzanne Fletcher
Publisher: Robert Watts

Series Information: **Sounds and Letters**

Credits
Photographs: Cover © NadyaEugene; p. 1 © bogdan ionescu, Irina oxilixo Danilova, abramsdesign, Subbotina Anna; p. 3 © Tsekhmister; p. 5 © Slatan; p. 7 © Realstockvector; p. 9 © ronstik; p. 11 © Frannyanne; p. 13 © Toey Toey; p. 15 © Olga Popova/Shutterstock.

Phonic support books are a wonderful resource for emergent readers as they encourage independent reading and help students make the link between letters and the sounds they represent.

Have students identify the images on the title page to listen for the long or short vowel sound that they will hear through the book.

Encourage students to point to each word as they read through the book.

ISBN: 9781922516756

**KNOWLEDGE
BOOKS**

Sounds&
Letters